Easy Travel Guide To Basel

A Stress-Free Exploration of Switzerland's Rich History, Stunning Architecture, and Hidden Gems

~Eva Lawson~

Copyright © 2024 by Eva Lawson

All rights reserved. No part of this travel guide may be reproduced, stored in a retrieval system, or transmitted in any form or by any means, electronic or mechanical, including photocopying, recording, or otherwise, without the prior written permission of the publisher, except for brief quotations used in book reviews. This travel guide aims to provide accurate and current information; however, details may change over time. We recommend verifying travel conditions, advisories, and local regulations to ensure a safe and enjoyable experience. Thank you for choosing this guide

Table of Contents

Introduction

Chapter 1 9
Welcome to Basel 9
An Overview 9
    Brief history and geography 11
    Best times to visit 13
    What makes Basel unique 16
Chapter 2 20
Getting There and Around 20
    Arriving in Basel 20
    By Air: 20
    By Rail: 22
    By Road: 23
    Public Transportation System 24
    Basel Card: 25
    Walking and Cycling in the City 26
    Cycling: 27
    Unique Transport Options: 28
Chapter 3 31
Where to Stay Accommodation Guide 31
    Budget-Friendly Options 32
    Mid-Range Hotels 34
    Luxury Accommodations 36
    Neighborhoods to Consider 38
Chapter 4 43

Basel's Must-See Attractions 43
    Old Town Highlights 44
    Basel Minster 47
    Museums and Galleries 48
    Rhine River Experiences 51

Chapter 5 57

Hidden Gems and Local Favorites 57
    Off-the-beaten-path Sites 57
    Local Markets and Shops 60
    Authentic Swiss Experiences 63
    Pro Tips for Authentic Experiences: ... 66

Chapter 6 69

Culinary Journey Through Basel 69
    Traditional Swiss Dishes to Try 70
    Best Restaurants for Every Budget 72
    Budget-Friendly Options: 72
    Mid-Range Restaurants: 73
    High-End Dining: 75
    Cafes and Bars 76
    Food Markets and Events 79
    Pro Tips for Basel Dining: 81

Chapter 7 85

Arts, Culture, and Festivals 85
    Basel's Vibrant Art Scene 86
    Annual Festivals and Events 89
    Theater and Music Venues 92
    Architecture Highlights 95
    Pro Tips for Culture Enthusiasts: 98

Chapter 8..101
Day Trips and Nearby Attractions............101
    Short Excursions from Basel 102
    Nature and Outdoor Activities............104
    Neighboring Towns Worth Visiting.....108
    Pro Tips for Day Trippers:..................111
Chapter 9..115
Practical Tips for a Smooth Visit 115
    Language Basics................................115
    Money Matters and Budgeting...........117
    Currency...117
    Budgeting Tips....................................118
    Money-Saving Tips.............................119
    Safety and Health Information 120
    Etiquette and Local Customs.............122
Conclusion...127
Making the Most of Your Basel Adventure 127

Introduction

Welcome to Basel

An Overview

Hey there, fellow adventurer! If you've picked up this book, you're in for a treat. Whether you're a culture enthusiast, a history buff, or just someone looking to explore one of Europe's most charming cities, you've made an excellent choice. Basel is waiting to surprise and delight you, and I'm here to be your friendly guide every step of the way.

You're not alone in this journey. Thousands of travelers discover the magic of Basel each year, and now you're part of that lucky group. This book is your key to unlocking the city's secrets, from its hidden gems to its must-see wonders. So take a deep breath, relax, and let's embark on this exciting adventure together!

Now, let's dive into what makes Basel truly special.

Brief history and geography

Nestled at the heart of Europe, where Switzerland, Germany, and France meet, Basel is a city that effortlessly blends the old with the new. Picture this: cobblestone streets winding through a medieval old town, all while cutting-edge architecture and world-class museums beckon around every corner. It's like stepping into a living, breathing storybook where history and innovation dance hand in hand.

Basel's story stretches back over 2,000 years. Founded by the Celts and later becoming a Roman outpost, the city has been a melting pot of cultures for centuries. During the Middle Ages, it flourished as a center of learning, home to Switzerland's oldest university (founded in 1460). The city's strategic location on the Rhine River helped it grow into a major trading hub, leaving us with the stunning merchant houses and grand buildings you'll see today.

Geographically, Basel is a gem. The mighty Rhine River cuts through the heart of the city, creating a natural divide between Grossbasel

(Greater Basel) on the south and west bank and Kleinbasel (Lesser Basel) on the north bank. Don't let the names fool you though – both sides have plenty to offer! The river isn't just pretty to look at; it's the lifeblood of the city, providing transportation, recreation, and a favorite spot for locals to relax on warm summer days.

Best times to visit

So, when's the best time to visit this Swiss wonderland? Honestly, Basel has something special to offer year-round, but let me break it down for you:

Spring (March to May) is absolutely magical. The city bursts into bloom, with parks and gardens showing off their colors. It's perfect for outdoor exploring, and you might catch the Basel Wine Fair in April if you're a wine enthusiast.

Summer (June to August) is when Basel really comes alive. The weather is warm and sunny, ideal for swimming in the Rhine or enjoying outdoor festivals. Don't miss the Basel Tattoo in July, a military music festival that'll knock your socks off.

Fall (September to November) brings a golden glow to the city. The crowds thin out, making it great for museum hopping. The Basel Autumn Fair in October is a centuries-old tradition you won't want to miss.

Winter (December to February) transforms Basel into a fairytale wonderland. The Christmas market is pure magic, and if you're lucky, you might see the city dusted with snow. February brings the famous

Fasnacht carnival, a three-day extravaganza that's unlike anything you've ever seen.

What makes Basel unique

Now, what makes Basel truly unique? It's not just one thing – it's a combination that you won't find anywhere else. Here's a taste:

1. Art at every turn: Basel isn't just a city with great museums (though it has plenty). It's a city where art is part of daily life. From sculptures in public squares to world-renowned Art Basel, creativity is in the city's DNA.

2. Three countries, one city: Where else can you have breakfast in Switzerland, lunch in France, and dinner in Germany? Basel's location at the "Three Countries Corner" makes for a one-of-a-kind cultural experience.

3. Architectural wonderland: Basel is home to buildings designed by more Pritzker Prize-winning architects than any other city. It's a playground for architecture buffs.

4. Rhine swimming culture: On hot summer days, locals pack their belongings in a Wickelfisch (a watertight fish-shaped bag) and float down the Rhine. It's a uniquely Basel experience you've got to try.

5. Fasnacht: Basel's carnival is so special it's on UNESCO's list of Intangible Cultural Heritage. It's 72 hours of music, parades, and traditions that date back centuries.

As we wrap up this chapter, I hope you're starting to feel the excitement building. Basel is a city that rewards the curious, delights the senses, and leaves you with memories that'll last a lifetime. In the coming chapters, we'll dig deeper into everything from where to stay and what to eat, to the hidden corners only locals know about.

So, are you ready to discover Basel? Let's go – your Swiss adventure awaits!

Chapter 2

Getting There and Around

Alright, savvy travelers, let's talk about how to reach Basel and navigate this charming city like a pro. Trust me, getting around Basel is half the fun, and I'm here to make sure you don't miss a beat.

Arriving in Basel

By Air:

EuroAirport Basel-Mulhouse-Freiburg is your gateway to the city. Now, here's where it gets interesting

- this airport is actually in France, but it has a Swiss sector. Don't worry, it's not as complicated as it sounds.

- From the airport, hop on bus 50 to the city center. It runs every 7-15 minutes and takes about 20 minutes to reach Basel SBB, the main train station.
- Alternatively, grab a taxi. It'll cost around 50 CHF and take about 15 minutes.
- **Pro tip:** When you land, head for the Swiss exit. This way, you'll enter Switzerland directly and won't need to go through French customs.

By Rail:

Basel SBB is a major European rail hub, making train travel a breeze.

- Direct trains connect Basel to major Swiss cities like Zurich (53 minutes), Bern (55 minutes), and Geneva (2 hours 41 minutes).
- International connections are plentiful. Paris is just 3 hours away, Frankfurt 3 hours, and Milan 4 hours.
- The station is right in the city center, with excellent public transport connections.

By Road:

Driving to Basel? You're in luck. The city is well-connected to the European motorway network.

- From Zurich, it's about an hour's drive on the A3.
- Coming from Germany? Take the A5 from Karlsruhe.
- If you're arriving from France, the A35 from Strasbourg will get you here.

Remember, to drive on Swiss motorways, you need a vignette (toll sticker). You can buy one at the border, gas stations, or post offices.

Public Transportation System

Basel's public transport system is a thing of beauty. It's efficient, extensive, and incredibly user-friendly.

Trams and Buses:
- The backbone of Basel's public transport is its tram network, supplemented by buses.
- Trams run from 5 am to around midnight, with night buses taking over on weekends.

- Buy tickets from machines at stops or use the BVB app for mobile tickets.
- A single ticket (valid for 30 minutes) costs 3.80 CHF. Day passes are available for 9.90 CHF.

Basel Card:

Here's a game-changer - all hotel guests receive a complimentary Basel Card. This gives you:
- Free use of public transport
- 50% off entry to Basel Zoo, museums, and theater performances
- Free Wi-Fi at 17 hotspots around the city

S-Bahn:

For exploring the wider Basel region, the S-Bahn (suburban rail) is your best friend. It connects Basel to surrounding areas in Switzerland, Germany, and France.

Walking and Cycling in the City

Walking:

Basel is a walker's paradise. The city center is compact and pedestrian-friendly.

- The Old Town is best explored on foot. Wander through narrow alleys and discover hidden squares.

- For a scenic stroll, follow the Rhine promenade from Kleinbasel to Grossbasel.

- **Free walking tours are available** - a great way to get oriented and learn some history.

Cycling:

Biking in Basel isn't just a mode of transport - it's a way of life.

- The city boasts over 130 km of cycle paths.

- Rent a bike through Pick-e-Bike or Donkey Republic apps. Prices start at around 3 CHF per hour.
- Basel Tourismus offers guided bike tours if you want to explore with an expert.
- Remember to lock your bike and use hand signals when turning.

Unique Transport Options:

- **Rhine Ferries:** For 1.60 CHF, cross the Rhine on one of four reaction ferries. They're powered solely by the river's current - a truly unique experience.

- **Basel Mobility Ticket:** If you're staying in Basel for a conference, you might receive this ticket, offering free public transport during your stay.

As we wrap up this chapter, remember that getting around Basel is part of the adventure. Whether you're gliding along on a tram, pedaling through picturesque streets, or letting the Rhine current guide your ferry, each journey is an opportunity to soak in the city's charm.

In our next chapter, we'll dive into where to rest your head after all this exploring. But for now, armed with this knowledge, you're ready to navigate Basel like a local. Happy travels!

This guide is packed with detailed insights, insider tips, and practical advice to help you make the most of your journey. To keep the Easy Travel Guide to Basel both affordable and accessible, we've prioritized valuable content over images. We believe that immersing yourself in Basel's rich history, stunning architecture, and hidden gems is far more rewarding than viewing them on a page. So, grab your map, plan your adventure, and get ready to explore Basel like never before!

Chapter 3

Where to Stay Accommodation Guide

Alright, travel enthusiasts, let's talk about one of the most crucial aspects of your Basel adventure - where you'll be resting your head at night. Basel offers a diverse range of accommodations to suit every taste and budget. From cozy hostels to luxurious hotels, we've got you covered. Let's dive in and find your perfect Basel home-away-from-home.

Budget-Friendly Options

Traveling on a shoestring? No worries - Basel has some great options that won't break the bank.

1. Youth Hostel Basel:

   - Located in St. Alban, this modern hostel offers dorms and private rooms.

   - Prices start from around 35 CHF per night for a dorm bed.

   - Perks include a communal kitchen and free public transport tickets.

2. YMCA Hostel Basel:

   - Centrally located near the train station.

- Dorm beds from 40 CHF, private rooms available.

- Includes breakfast and Basel Card.

3. Ibis Budget Basel City:

- Basic but clean rooms from 80 CHF per night.

- Located in Kleinbasel, close to the Rhine.

- No frills, but great value for money.

4. Hyve Hostel Basel:

- Modern hostel with a social atmosphere.

- Dorms from 35 CHF, private rooms available.

- Rooftop terrace with city views.

Pro tip: Book in advance, especially during peak seasons or events like Art Basel.

Mid-Range Hotels

For those with a bit more wiggle room in their budget, these mid-range options offer comfort without excessive splurging.

1. Hotel Spalentor:

- Charming 4-star hotel near the old city gate.

- Rooms from 150 CHF per night.

- Complimentary minibar and use of bicycles.

2. Motel One Basel:

- Modern design hotel near the SBB train station.

- Rooms from 120 CHF per night.

- Excellent breakfast and stylish lounge.

3. Hotel Rochat:

- Historic building in the Old Town.

- Rooms from 130 CHF per night.

- Quiet location, yet central.

4. Nomad Design & Lifestyle Hotel:

- Contemporary hotel with a unique vibe.
- Rooms from 160 CHF per night.
- Features a rooftop bar and sauna.

Luxury Accommodations

If you're looking to indulge, Basel has some truly spectacular high-end options.

1. Grand Hotel Les Trois Rois:

- Basel's most famous 5-star hotel, right on the Rhine.
- Rooms from 500 CHF per night.

- Three restaurants, including the 3-Michelin-starred Cheval Blanc.

2. Hotel Pullman Basel Europe:
- Modern luxury in the heart of the city.
- Rooms from 200 CHF per night.
- Excellent fitness center and Les Quatre Saisons restaurant.

3. Hyperion Hotel Basel:
- Sleek, contemporary hotel in Switzerland's tallest habitable building.
- Rooms from 180 CHF per night.
- Panoramic views from the 30th-floor bar.

4. Krafft Basel:

- Boutique luxury on the banks of the Rhine.

- Rooms from 230 CHF per night.

- Beautiful river views and acclaimed restaurant.

Neighborhoods to Consider

Choosing the right neighborhood can make or break your Basel experience. Here's a quick guide:

1. Altstadt Grossbasel (Old Town):

- Perfect for first-time visitors.

- Close to major attractions like the Münster and Marktplatz.

- Charming, but can be pricier and busier.

2. Kleinbasel:

- Across the Rhine, known for its alternative vibe.

- Great for nightlife and restaurants.

- Slightly more affordable than the Old Town.

3. St. Alban:

- Quiet, picturesque neighborhood.

- Home to the Paper Mill Museum and lovely riverside walks.
- Good for those seeking a more relaxed stay.

4. Gundeldingen:
- Multicultural area near the train station.
- More affordable accommodations.
- Great for experiencing local life.

5. St. Johann:
- Up-and-coming neighborhood with a young, creative vibe.
- Close to the Rhine and French border.

- Good mix of accommodation options.

Remember, no matter where you choose to stay, you'll receive a Basel Card with your accommodation, giving you free public transport and discounts on attractions. It's a fantastic perk that makes getting around the city a breeze.

A few final tips:
- Book early for big events like Art Basel or Fasnacht.
- Consider staying near a tram line for easy city access.

- Don't shy away from staying across the border in Germany or France - it can be more affordable, and you're still just a short tram ride from the city center.

Whether you're looking for a budget bunk or five-star luxury, Basel has a place for you. Sweet dreams, and get ready for the adventures that await in this beautiful city on the Rhine!

Chapter 4

Basel's Must-See Attractions

Welcome to the heart of your Basel adventure! This chapter is all about the can't-miss sights that make this city truly special. From medieval marvels to cutting-edge art, we're about to embark on a journey through Basel's most captivating attractions. Let's dive in and discover what makes this Swiss gem shine.

Old Town Highlights

Basel's Altstadt (Old Town) is a living museum, where every cobblestone tells a story. Here are the spots you absolutely must see:

1. Marktplatz and Rathaus (Town Hall):

   - The vibrant heart of Basel since the 14th century.
   - Don't miss the stunning red sandstone façade of the Rathaus.
   - Visit on Saturday mornings for the lively farmer's market.
   - Guided tours of the Rathaus available on Saturdays at 4:30 PM (book in advance).

✳ **2. Spalentor:**

- One of the best-preserved city gates in Switzerland.

- Dating back to the 14th century, it's a prime example of Basel's medieval fortifications.

- Climb to the top for a great view of the city (open April to October).

✲ **3. Tinguely Fountain:**

- A whimsical, kinetic sculpture by local artist Jean Tinguely.

- Located on the site of the old city theater.

- Best visited on a sunny day when the water features are in full swing.

✶ 4. Mittlere Brücke:

- Basel's oldest bridge, connecting Grossbasel and Kleinbasel.
- Originally built in 1226, it's been a crucial Rhine crossing for centuries.
- Great spot for photos, especially at sunset.

Pro tip: Join a free walking tour to get oriented and learn about the Old Town's rich history.

Basel Minster

The Basel Minster (Basler Münster) is more than just a church - it's the soul of the city.

- Gothic and Romanesque architectural styles blend beautifully in this 12th-century cathedral.
- Climb the 250 steps to the top of the tower for panoramic views of Basel and beyond (small fee applies).
- Don't miss the intricate carvings on the main portal and the vibrant roof tiles.
- Visit the cloister to see medieval tombstones and enjoy a moment of tranquility.

- **Opening hours:** Mon-Sat 10 AM - 5 PM, Sun 11:30 AM - 5 PM (tower closes 30 minutes before the church).

Insider tip: Time your visit for noon to hear the impressive bells ring out across the city.

Museums and Galleries

Basel is a cultural powerhouse, boasting over 40 museums in just 37 square kilometers. Here are some must-visits:

1. Kunstmuseum Basel:

- Switzerland's largest and most important public art collection.

- Houses works from the 15th century to present day.

- Don't miss the Holbein and van Gogh collections.

- Open Tue-Sun 10 AM - 6 PM (closed Mondays).

2. Fondation Beyeler:

- Modern and contemporary art in a stunning Renzo Piano-designed building.

- Located in Riehen, easily accessible by tram.

- Rotating exhibitions feature world-renowned artists.

- Open daily 10 AM - 6 PM (Wed until 8 PM).

3. Museum Tinguely:

- Dedicated to the kinetic sculptures of Jean Tinguely.
- Interactive and fun for all ages.
- Beautiful location on the Rhine.
- Open Tue-Sun 11 AM - 6 PM (closed Mondays).

4. Vitra Design Museum:

- Just across the border in Weil am Rhein, Germany.
- Showcases innovative furniture and interior design.

- The campus features buildings by star architects like Frank Gehry and Zaha Hadid.
- Open daily 10 AM - 6 PM.

Pro tip: Many museums offer free entry on the first Sunday of each month. The Basel Card also provides discounts on museum entry.

Rhine River Experiences

The Rhine is the lifeblood of Basel, and no visit is complete without experiencing its charm.

1. Rhine Swimming:

- A beloved local tradition during summer months.

- Join locals in floating down the river with a Wickelfisch (waterproof bag).

- Best entry point is at the Tinguely Museum.

- Always check current conditions and follow safety guidelines.

2. Rhine Ferries:

- Four reaction ferries cross the Rhine using only the current's power.

- A unique and eco-friendly way to cross the river.

- Each ride costs 1.60 CHF.

- Operating hours vary by season, generally from 11 AM until 5 PM (later in summer).

3. River Cruises:

- Several companies offer scenic cruises along the Rhine.
- Options range from short city tours to full-day trips to the Black Forest.
- Most cruises depart from Schifflände in the city center.
- Book in advance during peak summer months.

4. Riverside Walks:

- The promenade along Klein- and Grossbasel offers beautiful views.

- Perfect for a leisurely stroll or picnic.

- Don't miss the sunset from the Pfalz viewing terrace behind the Minster.

Remember, these attractions are just the beginning of what Basel has to offer. Each has its own unique charm and story to tell. As you explore, take time to soak in the atmosphere, chat with locals, and create your own Basel memories.

In our next chapter, we'll venture off the beaten path to discover some of Basel's hidden gems. But for now, enjoy these must-see sights - they're the essence of what makes Basel so special. Happy exploring!

This guide is packed with detailed insights, insider tips, and practical advice to help you make the most of your journey. To keep the Easy Travel Guide to Basel both affordable and accessible, we've prioritized valuable content over images. We believe that immersing yourself in Basel's rich history, stunning architecture, and hidden gems is far more rewarding than viewing them on a page. So, grab your map, plan your adventure, and get ready to explore Basel like never before!

Chapter 5

Hidden Gems and Local Favorites

Alright, intrepid explorers, it's time to peel back the layers of Basel and discover the city's best-kept secrets. In this chapter, we're venturing beyond the guidebook classics to uncover the spots that locals love and visitors often miss. Get ready to experience Basel like a true insider!

Off-the-beaten-path Sites

1. St. Alban-Tal (Little Venice): - A picturesque neighborhood known for its well-preserved medieval architecture.

- Home to Europe's oldest paper mill, now the Paper Museum.

- Take a stroll along the canals and admire the old waterwheels.

- Visit the Dalbe-Müli, a restored grain mill that still operates on special occasions.

2. Rehberger-Weg:

- A 5km art trail connecting Fondation Beyeler in Switzerland to Vitra Design Museum in Germany.

- Features 24 unique waymarkers designed by artist Tobias Rehberger.

- Perfect for a scenic walk or bike ride across three countries.

3. Münsterhügel Roman Ruins:
- Beneath Basel Minster lie the remains of a Roman fort.
- Access via the Archeological Museum (Tue-Sun, 10 AM - 5 PM).
- Offers a fascinating glimpse into Basel's ancient history.

4. Hörnli Cemetery:
- An unexpectedly beautiful spot with stunning views over Basel.
- Final resting place of cultural figures like art historian Jacob Burckhardt.

- Tranquil gardens perfect for a contemplative walk.

5. Workroom Warteck PP:
- A former brewery turned creative space.
- Home to artists' studios, exhibitions, and cultural events.
- Check their website for current happenings.

Local Markets and Shops

1. Markthalle:
- A renovated 1929 market hall housing international food stalls.

- Open Mon-Thu 8 AM - 8 PM, Fri-Sat 8 AM - 10 PM.
- Don't miss the craft beer bar in the central cupola.

2. Klybeckquai Flea Market:
- Held every Saturday (April-October) from 10 AM - 4 PM.
- Located along the Rhine in Kleinbasel.
- Great for vintage finds and local crafts.

3. Johann Wanner Christmas House: - World-famous Christmas decoration shop open year-round.

- Located in the Old Town at Spalenberg 14.

- Supplies ornaments to the Vatican and White House.

4. Läckerli Huus:

- The place to buy Basel's traditional hard spice cookies, Läckerli.

- Multiple locations, but visit the main store at Gerbergasse 57 for the full experience.

5. Von Bartha Gallery:

- Contemporary art gallery in a converted garage.

- Located in the residential area of Kannenfeldplatz.

- Showcases emerging and established artists.

Authentic Swiss Experiences

1. Basel Craft Beer Scene:

- Visit local breweries like Unser Bier or Kitchen Brew.

- Try "Ueli Bier" at Fischerstube, brewed on-site since 1974.

- Join a craft beer tour for a comprehensive taste of Basel's beer culture.

2. Herbschtmäss (Autumn Fair):

- Switzerland's oldest and largest fair, dating back to 1471.

- Held annually from late October to mid-November.
- Enjoy traditional foods, rides, and market stalls across the city.

3. Urban Gardening at Landhof:
- Community garden in a former sports stadium.
- Open to visitors; consider joining a gardening session if you're staying longer.
- Located in Kleinbasel, easily accessible by tram.

4. Hammam at Sauna am Rhy:
- Traditional Swiss sauna experience right on the Rhine.

- Open year-round, with outdoor pools overlooking the river.

- Check their website for women-only and mixed days.

5. Morgestraich:

- The 4 AM kick-off to Basel's famous Fasnacht carnival.

- Held on the Monday after Ash Wednesday.

- Experience the city plunged into darkness, lit only by carnival lanterns.

6. Basel Wine Tasting:

- Visit Buess Weinbau in Aesch, just outside Basel.

- Family-run vineyard offering tours and tastings of local wines.

- Reservation required, easily reached by S-Bahn.

Pro Tips for Authentic Experiences:

1. Learn a few words of Baseldytsch, the local dialect. Even a simple "Merci vielmal" (thank you very much) will win you smiles.

2. Join a local Meetup group or check couchsurfing.com for events to meet Basel residents.

3. Explore the city by bike - it's how many locals get around and offers a different perspective.

4. Visit a traditional Beiz (pub) like Gifthüttli or Brauner Mutz for a truly local evening out.

5. Take a dip in the Rhybadhysli St. Johann, a historic river swimming facility that's a favorite among locals.

Remember, some of the best experiences in Basel come from simply wandering the streets, chatting with locals, and being open to unexpected discoveries. Don't be afraid to venture into residential neighborhoods or ask locals for their favorite spots - Baslers are generally friendly and happy to share their city's secrets.

By exploring these hidden gems and local favorites, you'll gain a deeper appreciation for Basel's unique character and create memories that go beyond the typical tourist experience. So go ahead, dive in, and uncover the Basel that locals know and love. Your adventure awaits!

Chapter 6

Culinary Journey Through Basel

Welcome, food lovers! Get ready to embark on a mouthwatering adventure through Basel's vibrant culinary scene. From traditional Swiss delicacies to international fusion, this city's gastronomic offerings are sure to tantalize your taste buds. Let's dive into the flavors that make Basel a true foodie paradise.

Traditional Swiss Dishes to Try

1. Basler Läckerli: - Hard spice cookies originating from Basel.

 - Made with honey, hazelnuts, and candied peel.

 - Best enjoyed with a cup of coffee or tea.

2. Basler Mehlsuppe:

 - A hearty flour soup traditionally served during Fasnacht.

 - Rich, savory, and perfect for cold days.

3. Käsewähe:

 - Swiss cheese tart, similar to quiche but with a thinner crust.

- Often enjoyed as a snack or light meal.

4. Raclette:
- Melted cheese scraped onto potatoes, pickles, and bread.
- A social dish, often enjoyed in groups.

5. Fondue:
- While more associated with other parts of Switzerland, it's still popular in Basel.
- Try cheese fondue or, for dessert, chocolate fondue.

6. Rösti:

- A crispy potato pancake, often served with various toppings.

- Makes for a delicious breakfast or side dish.

Best Restaurants for Every Budget

Budget-Friendly Options:

1. Tibits:

- Vegetarian and vegan buffet.

- Pay by weight, so you can control your spending.

- Located near the SBB station.

2. Zum Goldenen Fass:

- Traditional Swiss cuisine in a cozy setting.

- Known for their reasonably priced daily menus.

- Located in Kleinbasel.

3. Lily's Stomach Supply:

- Asian fusion street food.

- Popular among locals for quick, tasty meals.

- Two locations: one near Barfüsserplatz and one in Kleinbasel.

Mid-Range Restaurants:

1. Kunsthalle Restaurant:

- Beautiful garden terrace in summer.
- Mix of Swiss and international cuisine.
- Located near the Kunstmuseum.

2. Volkshaus Basel:
- Modern Swiss cuisine in a trendy setting.
- Also hosts cultural events and concerts.
- Located in Kleinbasel.

3. Walliser Kanne:
- Specializes in fondue and raclette.
- Cozy, traditional Swiss atmosphere.

- Located in the Old Town.

High-End Dining:

1. Cheval Blanc:

- 3 Michelin stars, led by chef Peter Knogl.
- French haute cuisine with Mediterranean and Asian influences.
- Located in the Grand Hotel Les Trois Rois.

2. Stucki:

- 2 Michelin stars, helmed by chef Tanja Grandits.

- Known for innovative flavor combinations.

- Located in a beautiful villa in Bruderholz.

3. Bel Etage:

- 1 Michelin star, focusing on modern European cuisine.

- Elegant dining room with views of the Rhine.

- Located in Der Teufelhof Basel hotel.

Cafes and Bars

Cafes:

1. Confiserie Schiesser:

- Basel's oldest café, dating back to 1870.
- Famous for their pastries and hot chocolate.
- Located on Marktplatz.

2. Zum Kuss:
- Hip café in a former public toilet building.
- Great for people-watching on Barfüsserplatz.

3. Merian Gärten Café:
- Serene café in beautiful botanical gardens.
- Perfect for a peaceful break from city exploring.

Bars:

1. Bar Rouge: - Cocktail bar with panoramic views from the 31st floor.

- Located in the Messeturm.

2. Consum:

- Wine bar with an extensive selection of local and international wines.
- Also offers delicious tapas.
- Located in the Old Town.

3. Cargo Bar:

- Trendy bar right on the Rhine.

- Popular spot for summer drinks on the terrace.

- Located in Kleinbasel.

Food Markets and Events

1. Marktplatz Farmer's Market:

- Held every weekday morning until 1 PM.

- Best on Saturdays when it's largest.

- Fresh local produce, flowers, and specialty foods.

2. Street Food Festival Basel:

- Held annually in August.

- Features a wide variety of international cuisines.
- Located at Kohlistieg in Kleinbasel.

3. Basel Wine Fair: - Annual event in October/November.
- Opportunity to taste wines from the Basel region and beyond.
- Held at Messe Basel.

4. Basel Gourmet Festival:
- Week-long celebration of fine dining held annually.
- Features guest chefs from around the world.

- Various locations throughout the city.

5. Markthalle:

- Year-round indoor market with international food stalls.
- Open Monday to Saturday.
- Great for lunch or picking up specialty ingredients.

Pro Tips for Basel Dining:

1. Reservations are recommended for higher-end restaurants, especially on weekends.

2. Many restaurants offer a daily "Menu" or "Tageskarte" - a set lunch menu that's often great value.

3. Tipping is not mandatory in Switzerland as service is included, but rounding up or adding 5-10% for good service is appreciated.

4. Try local Basel wines - the region produces excellent Pinot Noir and Müller-Thurgau.

5. Don't be surprised by early closing times - many kitchens close by 10 PM, even on weekends.

6. For a unique experience, try dining in the dark at Blindekuh Basel, where visually impaired staff guide you through a meal in complete darkness.

Remember, Basel's culinary scene is constantly evolving, with new restaurants and food trends emerging regularly. Don't be afraid to ask locals for their current favorites - Baslers are often eager to share their gastronomic discoveries.

From traditional Swiss comfort food to cutting-edge cuisine, Basel offers a feast for every palate and budget. So loosen your belt and prepare for a delicious journey through this city's diverse and delightful food landscape. Bon appétit, or as they say in Basel, **"E Guete"**!

Chapter 7

Arts, Culture, and Festivals

Welcome to the beating heart of Basel's cultural scene! This Swiss city may be compact, but it packs a mighty punch when it comes to arts and culture. From world-class museums to quirky festivals, Basel offers a rich tapestry of experiences that will captivate any culture enthusiast. Let's dive into the creative spirit that makes this city truly special.

Basel's Vibrant Art Scene

Basel is often called the cultural capital of Switzerland, and for good reason. The city boasts an impressive array of museums and galleries that cater to all tastes.

1. Art Basel:

  - The world's premier international art fair, held annually in June.

  - Attracts over 90,000 visitors and features works from top galleries worldwide.

  - Tip: Book accommodations well in advance if visiting during this time.

2. Kunstmuseum Basel: - The oldest public art collection in the world, dating back to 1661.
  - Houses works from the 15th century to contemporary art.
  - Don't miss the Holbein and van Gogh collections.
  - Open Tue-Sun, 10 AM - 6 PM.

3. Fondation Beyeler:
  - Modern and contemporary art in a stunning Renzo Piano-designed building.
  - Rotating exhibitions feature world-renowned artists.
  - Located in Richen, easily accessible by tram.

- Open daily, 10 AM - 6 PM (Wed until 8 PM).

4. Museum Tinguely:
   - Dedicated to the kinetic sculptures of Jean Tinguely.
   - Interactive and fun for all ages.
   - Beautiful location on the Rhine.
   - Open Tue-Sun, 11 AM - 6 PM.

5. Schaulager:
   - Unique combination of public museum, art storage facility, and research institute.
   - Open to the public during special exhibitions.

- Located in Münchenstein, reachable by tram.

Annual Festivals and Events

Basel's calendar is packed with festivals and events that showcase the city's cultural diversity and zest for life.

1. Fasnacht (Basel Carnival):

- Switzerland's largest carnival, typically held in February or March.

- Features elaborate costumes, parades, and traditional "Gugge" music.

- Starts with "Morgestraich" at 4 AM on Monday after Ash Wednesday.

- Tip: Book accommodations far in advance for this popular event.

2. Basel Tattoo:

- World's second-largest military music festival.

- Held annually in July at the barracks courtyard.

- Features performances from international military bands and display teams.

3. Culturescapes:-
Multidisciplinary festival focusing

on a different country or region each year.

- Held in autumn, featuring music, theater, dance, and visual arts.

4. Basel Autumn Fair (Basler Herbstmesse):

- Switzerland's oldest and largest fair, dating back to 1471.
- Held from late October to mid-November across various city locations.
- Enjoy traditional foods, rides, and market stalls.

5. Basel Christmas Market: - One of the prettiest and largest Christmas markets in Switzerland.

- Held from late November to December 23rd.

- Located on Barfüsserplatz and Münsterplatz.

Theater and Music Venues

Basel's performing arts scene is vibrant and diverse, offering everything from classical concerts to avant-garde theater.

1. Theater Basel:

- The largest multi-purpose theater in Switzerland.

- Offers opera, ballet, and drama performances.

- Located near Barfüsserplatz.

- **Tip:** English surtitles are often available for opera performances.

2. Stadtcasino Basel:

- One of the oldest and most important concert halls in Europe.

- Home to the Basel Symphony Orchestra.

- Recently renovated, reopened in 2020.

- Located in the city center.

Kaserne Basel: - Contemporary performing arts center in a former barracks.
   - Hosts dance, theater, and music performances.
   - Located in Kleinbasel.

4. Bird's Eye Jazz Club:
   - Intimate venue featuring local and international jazz artists.
   - Located in the Old Town.
   - Performances usually start at 8:30 PM.

5. Gare du Nord:
   - Venue for contemporary music and experimental performances.

- Located in a former train station in Basel's north.

Architecture Highlights

Basel is a treasure trove of architectural gems, blending medieval charm with cutting-edge modern design.

1. Basel Minster:
 - Romanesque-Gothic cathedral dating back to the 12th century.
 - Climb the tower for panoramic views of the city.

2. Rathaus (Town Hall):
 - 16th-century red sandstone building in the Marktplatz.

- Features beautiful frescoes and a picturesque courtyard.

3. Spalentor:
  - One of the most beautiful and well-preserved city gates in Switzerland.
  - Built in the 14th century as part of the city's fortifications.

4. Roche Tower:
  - Switzerland's tallest building at 178 meters.
  - Designed by Herzog & de Meuron, completed in 2015.

5. Vitra Design Museum:-
Located just across the border in Weil am Rhein, Germany.

- Campus features buildings by star architects like Frank Gehry and Zaha Hadid.

6. Novartis Campus:

- Collection of buildings designed by world-renowned architects.

- Note: The campus is not open to the public, but guided tours are occasionally available.

Pro Tips for Culture Enthusiasts:

1. Check out the "Museumspass" for unlimited entry to many museums in Basel and the surrounding region.

2. Many museums offer free entry on the first Sunday of each month.

3. The Basel Card, provided with your hotel stay, offers discounts on many cultural attractions.

4. For up-to-date event listings, check out www.basel.com or pick up a copy of the local "Basel Agenda" magazine.

5. Don't overlook smaller galleries and performance spaces - they often showcase exciting local talent.

Basel's cultural scene is constantly evolving, with new exhibitions, performances, and events popping up regularly. Whether you're an art aficionado, a history buff, or simply curious about Swiss culture, Basel offers a wealth of experiences to explore. So dive in, let your curiosity guide you, and prepare to be inspired by this city's rich cultural tapestry. Enjoy your cultural journey through Basel!

Chapter 8

Day Trips and Nearby Attractions

While Basel itself is a treasure trove of experiences, the surrounding region offers even more adventures for the curious traveler. From picturesque villages to stunning natural landscapes, there's a wealth of attractions just a short journey from the city. Let's explore some of the best day trips and nearby attractions that will add depth and variety to your Basel adventure.

Short Excursions from Basel

1. Augusta Raurica:

- Ancient Roman colony and archaeological site.
- Located about 20 km east of Basel in Augst.
- Features well-preserved ruins, including a theater and forum.
- Open daily, 10 AM - 5 PM (April-September) and 11 AM - 4 PM (October-March).
- Easily accessible by train from Basel SBB (20-minute ride).

2. Rheinfelden:

- Charming Swiss town on the Rhine, known for its saline baths.

- Home to Switzerland's oldest brewery, Feldschlösschen.

- Just 15 minutes by train from Basel.

- Don't miss the picturesque Old Town and the covered wooden bridge.

3. Laufenburg:

- Medieval town straddling the Swiss-German border.

- Known for its beautiful Old Town and castle ruins.

- About 30 minutes by train from Basel.

- Great spot for a leisurely lunch and a stroll along the Rhine.

4. Solothurn:

- Often called Switzerland's most beautiful Baroque city.
- Home to 11 museums and the impressive St. Ursus Cathedral.
- About an hour by train from Basel.
- Visit on a Saturday to experience the vibrant weekly market.

Nature and Outdoor Activities

1. Jura Mountains:

- Perfect for hiking, mountain biking, and winter sports.

- The Wasserfallen cable car offers easy access to hiking trails.

- About an hour from Basel by public transport.

- Don't miss the panoramic views from Passwang or Belchenflue.

2. Black Forest, Germany:

- Famous for its dense evergreen forests and picturesque villages.

- Great for hiking, especially the Schluchtensteig trail.

- Try the famous Black Forest cake in its place of origin.

- Accessible by car (about 1 hour) or organized tours from Basel.

3. Rhine Falls:
- Europe's largest plain waterfall.
- Located near Schaffhausen, about 1.5 hours by train from Basel.
- Take a boat ride to get up close to the falls.
- Best visited in late spring or early summer when water flow is at its peak.

4. Creux du Van:
- Natural rock arena with cliffs over 160 meters high.

- Excellent for hiking and wildlife spotting (ibex and marmots).
- About 2 hours from Basel by car.
- Offers breathtaking views of the Alps and Jura mountains.

5. Lake Lucerne:
- Stunning lake surrounded by mountains.
- Options for boat cruises, swimming, and water sports.
- About 1.5 hours by train from Basel.
- Visit Mount Pilatus or Rigi for panoramic views.

Neighboring Towns Worth Visiting

1. Colmar, France: - Picturesque Alsatian town known for its well-preserved old town.

 - Famous for its colorful half-timbered houses and canals.

 - About 1 hour by train from Basel.

 - Don't miss the Unterlinden Museum and the "Little Venice" quarter.

2. Freiburg, Germany:

 - Charming university town in the Black Forest.

- Known for its medieval old town and progressive environmental policies.

- About 1 hour by train from Basel.

- Visit the magnificent Freiburg Minster and enjoy the lively atmosphere around Augustinerplatz.

3. Mulhouse, France:

- Industrial town with several world-class museums.

- Home to the National Automobile Museum and the European Train Museum.

- Just 30 minutes by train from Basel.

- Great destination for transport enthusiasts.

4. Bern:

- Switzerland's capital city, known for its medieval old town (a UNESCO World Heritage site).

- Home to the famous Zytglogge clock tower and Einstein's house.

- About 1 hour by train from Basel.

- Don't miss the Bear Park and the panoramic views from the Rose Garden.

5. Zurich:

- Switzerland's largest city and financial hub.
- Offers a mix of historical charm and modern urban life.
- Just 1 hour by train from Basel.
- Explore the Old Town, take a boat trip on Lake Zurich, or enjoy the vibrant cultural scene.

Pro Tips for Day Trippers:

1. Consider purchasing a Swiss Travel Pass if you plan on taking multiple day trips by train. It offers unlimited travel on trains, buses, and boats.

2. Many of these destinations are included in the Swiss Museum Pass, which can save you money if you plan to visit several museums.

3. Always check the weather forecast before heading out, especially for outdoor activities in the mountains.

4. For trips to France or Germany, remember to bring your passport as you'll be crossing international borders.

5. Some smaller towns may have limited dining options on Sundays and public holidays, so plan accordingly.

6. Consider joining organized tours for more distant destinations like the Black Forest or Rhine Falls. They often include transportation and guided experiences.

These day trips offer a perfect complement to your Basel stay, allowing you to experience the diverse landscapes, cultures, and attractions of the tri-border region. Whether you're interested in history, nature, or simply exploring charming towns, there's something for everyone just a short journey from Basel. So pack a day bag, hop on a train, and get ready to broaden your Swiss adventure beyond the city limits. **Happy exploring!**

Chapter 9

Practical Tips for a Smooth Visit

Welcome to the practical side of your Basel adventure! In this chapter, we'll cover all the essential information you need to navigate the city like a pro. From language basics to local customs, we've got you covered. Let's dive in and make sure your trip to Basel is as smooth as Swiss chocolate.

Language Basics

While Basel is a multilingual city, the primary language spoken is Swiss

German. Don't worry, though – many locals are proficient in High German and English, especially in tourist areas. Here are some key phrases to help you get by:

- **Hello:** Grüezi (formal) or Hoi (informal)
- **Thank you:** Merci or Danke
- **Please:** Bitte
- **Yes:** Ja
- **No:** Nein
- **Excuse me:** Entschuldigung
- **Do you speak English?:** Sprechen Sie Englisch?
- **Cheers (for toasting):** Prost!

Pro tip: Even if you're not fluent, locals appreciate when visitors make an effort to use some basic German phrases. It's a great ice-breaker and often leads to friendly conversations.

Money Matters and Budgeting

Switzerland is known for being expensive, but with some smart planning, you can enjoy Basel without breaking the bank.

Currency

The official currency is the Swiss Franc (CHF). While some places accept Euros, it's best to use Swiss Francs for the most favorable exchange rates.

Budgeting Tips

1. Accommodation: Expect to spend 100-200 CHF per night for a mid-range hotel. Budget options like hostels start around 30-50 CHF per night.

2. Food: A meal at an inexpensive restaurant costs about 20-25 CHF, while a three-course meal at a mid-range restaurant might be 70-100 CHF for two people.

3. Transportation: A single ticket for public transport costs about 3-4 CHF. Consider a day pass (around 8-10 CHF) if you plan to use public transport frequently.

4. Attractions: Many museums offer free entry on the first Sunday of each month. The Basel Card, which you receive for free when staying at a hotel, offers free public transport and 50% off many attractions.

Money-Saving Tips

- Take advantage of the many free walking tours available.

- Shop at local markets and supermarkets for picnic supplies.
- Look for lunch specials at restaurants, which are often cheaper than dinner menus.
- Use tap water – it's safe to drink and free!

Safety and Health Information

Basel is generally a very safe city, but it's always good to be prepared.

Safety Tips

1. Be aware of your surroundings, especially in crowded tourist areas.

2. Keep your valuables secure and be cautious with your belongings in public places.

3. Use official taxis or reputable ride-sharing services, especially at night.

4. The emergency number for police, fire, or ambulance in Switzerland is 112.

Health Information

1. Switzerland has excellent healthcare facilities, but they can be expensive. Ensure you have comprehensive travel insurance before your trip.

2. Pharmacies (Apotheke) are widely available and can offer advice for minor health issues.

3. If you need a doctor, ask your hotel for recommendations or call 061 261 15 15 for the medical emergency service.

4. Tap water is safe to drink throughout Basel.

Etiquette and Local Customs

Swiss culture values politeness, punctuality, and respect for privacy. Here are some tips to help you blend in:

1. Greetings: A handshake is the most common greeting. Among friends, it's common to give three kisses on the cheek (left-right-left).

2. Punctuality: The Swiss take punctuality seriously. Arrive on time for appointments, tours, and restaurant reservations.

3. Quiet hours: Respect quiet hours, typically from 10 PM to 7 AM. Avoid loud noises during these times, especially in residential areas.

4. Recycling: The Swiss are environmentally conscious. Use the appropriate recycling bins for different materials.

5. Tipping: Service charges are usually included in restaurant bills. If you're particularly pleased with the service, rounding up or adding 5-10% is appreciated but not expected.

6. Public transport: Wait for passengers to exit before boarding, and offer your seat to elderly or pregnant passengers.

7. Photography: Always ask permission before photographing individuals, especially in markets or small shops.

8. Dining etiquette: Keep your hands visible on the table while eating, not in your lap. It's polite to finish everything on your plate.

Remember, these customs might differ slightly from what you're used to, but embracing them will enhance your experience and show respect for the local culture.

By keeping these practical tips in mind, you'll be well-prepared to enjoy all that Basel has to offer.

From navigating the language to understanding local customs, you're now equipped to explore this beautiful Swiss city with confidence. Enjoy your adventure in Basel!

Conclusion

Making the Most of Your Basel Adventure

As we wrap up our journey through the enchanting city of Basel, it's clear that this Swiss gem offers a treasure trove of experiences waiting to be discovered. From its rich history and stunning architecture to its vibrant cultural scene and hidden local spots, Basel is a city that rewards the curious traveler at every turn.

Remember, the true magic of Basel lies not just in its world-renowned museums or picturesque Old Town, but in the small moments that make your trip uniquely yours. Perhaps it's the warm smile of a local shopkeeper as you practice your newly learned Swiss German phrases, or the unexpected beauty of stumbling upon a quiet courtyard off the beaten path. These are the moments that transform a good trip into an unforgettable adventure.

As you plan your visit, keep in mind the practical tips we've shared throughout this guide. They'll help you navigate the city with confidence, leaving you free to focus on soaking in the experiences that await you. Whether you're sampling local delicacies at the Marktplatz, marveling at the masterpieces in the Kunstmuseum, or simply watching the world go by from a café along the Rhine, remember to take a moment to appreciate the unique blend of old-world charm and modern vibrancy that makes Basel so special.

Don't be afraid to step out of your comfort zone. Strike up a conversation with locals at a neighborhood bar, join a guided tour to dig deeper into the city's fascinating history, or venture out to explore the nearby Black Forest or Alsace region. Basel's central location makes it an ideal base for discovering the heart of Europe.

For families, couples, solo travelers, and everyone in between, Basel offers a wealth of experiences tailored to your interests. The city's compact size and efficient public transport system make it easy to pack your days full of activities, or to take it slow and savor each moment – the choice is yours.

As you embark on your Basel adventure, keep an open mind and a willingness to embrace the unexpected. Let the city's unique rhythm guide you, whether it's the gentle lapping of the Rhine against ancient stone walls or the cheerful chiming of church bells echoing through narrow streets.

Remember, travel is as much about the journey as it is the destination. In Basel, you'll find a perfect blend of Swiss efficiency and laid-back charm, creating an ideal backdrop for your own personal adventure story. From the moment you arrive until long after you've returned home, Basel will captivate your imagination and leave you with memories to cherish for a lifetime.

So pack your bags, bring your sense of wonder, and prepare to fall in love with Basel. Whether this is your first visit or your tenth, the city always has something new to offer. Who knows? You might just find yourself planning your return trip before you've even left.

Here's to new experiences, cultural discoveries, and the joy of exploration. Basel awaits – are you ready for the adventure of a lifetime?

Bon voyage, safe travels, and most importantly, enjoy every moment of your Basel experience!

Printed in Great Britain
by Amazon